John Adams ★ Abigail Adams

Two Biographies

by Christina Wilsdon

Table of Contents

BIOGRAPHY

What is a biography?

A biography is a factual retelling of another person's life. The person may have lived long ago or in recent history, or the person may still be alive today. Biographies can cover a person's entire life, or just important parts of a person's life. When possible, a biography includes direct quotes from the person. This helps the reader make a connection to the person.

What is the purpose of a biography?

A biography helps a reader understand the people, places, times, and events that were or are important in the subject's life. It provides a summary of the person's major life experiences and achievements. In addition, the way the author writes the biography helps a reader get a sense of the person as a real human being who had (and perhaps still has) an impact on the lives of others.

How do you read a biography?

The title will tell you the subject of the biography and may include something interesting about him or her. The first paragraph will try to "hook" the reader by capturing his or her attention. As you read, note the setting. The setting often influences what happens in a person's life. Also pay close attention to the sequence of events in the person's life. Ask yourself: *Did this event happen to the person, or did the person make it happen? How did this event affect the person's life? What do I admire about this person? Is there something in this person's experiences that I could apply to my life?*

A biography tells the person's date and place of birth.

A biography tells about the person's family, childhood, and important events.

A biography starts with a strong "hook."

Features of a Biography

A biography describes the person's impact on the world.

A biography describes the person's personality and characteristics.

A biography quotes the person and/or people who knew the person.

Who writes biographies?

People who write biographies want to learn more about others' life stories and how those people made their marks on the world. Some people write biographies because they are interested in a certain topic, such as sports, history, or cooking. Others write biographies simply because they are interested in people!

Tools for Readers and Writers

Direct Quotes

Authors of biographies want to help their readers understand the subject's personality. To show what the person is (or was) like, the author might interview the subject or people who know the subject. Sometimes, the author will include quotes from these interviews or from the subject's published and unpublished writing or speeches (for example, letters, diaries, recordings, and film or video clips). Quotations from these sources are called direct quotes.

Direct quotes provide first-hand information about the person and his or her story. Including such quotes gives readers a feel for the person and his or her character traits and helps them make inferences and draw conclusions about the subject. Direct quotes also establish that the author has "done his homework," writes with authority about the subject, and can be trusted.

Emotion Words

Writers use emotion words to express the feelings of characters or real people. These words convey a strong feeling or belief about certain events, other people, laws, war, and more. The words help reveal an individual's personality and thoughts and also help bring a story alive for the reader.

Text Structure and Organization

Authors put words together in several ways called text structures or patterns. These text structures include compare and contrast, cause and effect, problem and solution, sequence of events or steps in a process, and description. In many cases, authors use key words and phrases that help readers determine the text structure being used but in some cases, the reader has to think about the text's structure. Knowing how the author organized the events, ideas, and information in the text helps the reader understand and remember what was read.

Meet the Subjects
John Adams and Abigail Adams

John Adams

was a "Founding Father" of the United States and the country's second president.

- Born October 30, 1735, in Braintree, Massachusetts
- Died July 4, 1826, age ninety-one

Abigail Adams

was John Adams's wife and a key, behind-the-scenes political advisor.

- Born Abigail Smith on November 11, 1744, in Weymouth, Massachusetts
- Died October 28, 1818, age seventy-three

John Adams

John's childhood home in Quincy, Massachusetts, is part of Adams National Historical Park. During his lifetime, the town was called Braintree.

The jaws of power are always open to devour . . . to destroy the freedom of thinking, speaking, and writing." John Adams wrote these words in 1765, when the American colonies simmered with anger at laws passed by their ruling country, Great Britain. John and many other colonists thought the laws were unfair.

Disagreements between Great Britain and the colonies grew over the next ten years. They turned into scattered battles, then full-blown war by 1776. During this troubled time, John fought for American independence and, in his words, "the cause of truth, of virtue, of liberty, and of humanity."

Farm Boy

John was born on October 30, 1735, in Braintree, Massachusetts. His home was a simple farmhouse shared with his parents and two younger brothers.

John's father was a farmer, shoemaker, and church leader. John admired him greatly and planned to be a farmer, too. But John's father wanted him to go to college.

Young John, however, had little interest in school. He loved to read the books that filled the little house, but he did not like the **irritable** teacher in the town's one-room schoolhouse. He often skipped school to swim, fish, and fly kites. So John's father sent him to a private tutor. John regained his love of learning and was ready to go to Harvard College when he turned fifteen.

From Schoolroom to Courtroom

After graduating in 1755, John took a job teaching school. He studied law on the side. In 1758, he opened his own law office. His work required him to travel widely, on horseback, to visit different courts.

In 1761, John watched a Boston lawyer argue against a law that allowed British officials to freely enter homes, offices, and warehouses to search for smuggled goods. In his speech, the lawyer declared that colonists were entitled to the rights of "life, liberty, and property." John was very impressed. He later recalled, "Then and there the child Independence was born."

Tense Times

In October 1764, John married Abigail Smith. Abigail, like John, had a keen mind. The two enjoyed discussing politics. There were certainly many issues to discuss, such as the Sugar Act passed by the British Parliament earlier that year.

The Sugar Act was a tax on sugar intended to pay for the British army's protection of the colonies. But many people were angry because the colonies did not have representatives in Parliament. "No taxation without representation," they demanded. John agreed.

In 1765, Great Britain **enraged** colonists again by passing the Stamp Act. This law put a tax on all newspapers, contracts, and other material printed in the colonies. Many colonists refused to use the stamps. British tax collectors were attacked. Riots broke out in the streets.

John frowned on the riots, but he was against the Stamp Act. He called it "that enormous engine, fabricated by the British Parliament, for battering down all the Rights and Liberties of America." He shared his ideas about democracy, rights, and government by writing newspaper articles and essays.

The Stamp Act was repealed in 1766. But in 1767, taxes were placed on tea, glass, and other goods imported into the colonies. Many colonists responded by boycotting British imports.

John considered himself a patriot and approved of the boycott, but not of attacks on British officials. He defended the nine British soldiers charged with shooting five colonial protesters on March 5, 1770—an event known as the Boston Massacre.

John knew that defending the soldiers would make him unpopular. But he felt it was important to show Great Britain that colonists respected fair laws. He knew the protesters had threatened the soldiers and thrown rocks and ice at them. The soldiers, he felt, deserved a fair trial. In the end, only two of the soldiers were found guilty of manslaughter.

Though many people were **dismayed** by John's action, they still respected him greatly. They elected him to the Massachusetts state government in June 1770.

Patriot Paul Revere created a picture of the Boston Massacre that was exciting but not accurate. It added fuel to the fire of anti-British feelings.

Rebellion Grows

On the night of December 16, 1773, a band of patriots slipped aboard cargo ships in Boston Harbor. They threw 342 crates of tea into the water to protest the British tax on tea.

The Boston Tea Party

John was delighted when he heard about the Boston Tea Party. "This is the most magnificent Movement of all. There is a Dignity . . . in this last Effort of the Patriots, that I greatly admire," he wrote.

Furious, the British government closed Boston's port and shut off all trade. Town meetings were made illegal. A British general arrived to govern Massachusetts. The colonies responded by planning a meeting of representatives from each colony—the First Continental Congress. John was picked to be a representative.

Demand for Independence

In September 1774 and again in May 1775, John traveled to Philadelphia, Pennsylvania, to attend the First Continental Congress. He urged other delegates to stop trying to compromise with Great Britain and to support independence. America, he felt, had "nothing to hope for from our loving Mother Country."

John also pushed for the creation of an American army and nominated George Washington to lead it. Busy as he was, John

This painting, *Declaration of Independence*, hangs in the rotunda of the U.S. Capitol. John stands in the center, with his hand on his hip.

also worked with Thomas Jefferson to write the Declaration of Independence, which became official on July 4, 1776.

John was thrilled, but also **somber**. "I am well aware of the toil and blood and treasure that it will cost us to maintain this Declaration and support and defend these States," he wrote. "Yet, through all the gloom, I can see the rays of ravishing light and glory."

There was still one last chance to avoid war. John and two other men tried to discuss a peaceful solution with British army leaders in September 1776. But when John learned he would not be treated as a representative of a new nation, he replied, "Your lordship may consider me, in what light you please . . . except that of a British subject."

There would be no peace. America was officially at war.

War and Peace

John was put in charge of America's war committee. It was his job to supply the Continental Army with everything from boots to gunpowder. But after a year of war, money and supplies ran low. So in February 1778, John sailed to France to join Benjamin Franklin in asking for help. France agreed to provide money, soldiers, and ships.

John returned to Massachusetts in 1779. During his short visit home, he wrote a constitution for Massachusetts, setting out rules of government. The U.S. Constitution is based on John's document.

Later that year, John sailed back to Europe to start planning a peace treaty with Great Britain. But war raged for nearly two more years. During this time, John traveled to the Netherlands to urge that nation to recognize America's independence and to loan it money.

In this unfinished painting, John (seated at left) is shown at the signing of a peace treaty between Great Britain and the United States in 1783. Benjamin Franklin sits next to him.

Finally, on October 19, 1781, Great Britain surrendered. John threw himself into crafting a peace treaty. It took nearly two years before it was signed on September 3, 1783.

At long last, the War of Independence was over. John's time in Europe, however, was not. He stayed to work as America's representative in Great Britain. Abigail and their daughter, Nabby, sailed to Europe in 1784 to join him.

Vice President to President

In the summer of 1788, the Adamses returned to America. Cheering crowds welcomed them home. John was glad to be back on his farm. That very autumn, however, he ran in the nation's first presidential election.

At that time, candidates did not team up to run for election as president and vice president. George Washington won and became president. John became vice president by finishing second.

John was ready to work hard, but he quickly grew **frustrated**. His strong opinions clashed with those of the men in Washington's cabinet. He called the vice presidency "the most insignificant office that ever the invention of man contrived."

In 1796, Washington decided not to run for re-election. This time, John squeaked out a narrow victory and became the nation's second president. Thomas Jefferson became vice president.

The two men made an odd pair, for they disagreed hotly with each other. They especially locked horns when they discussed France and Great Britain, which started warring in 1793.

France insisted that the United States should help them fight. Some Americans, including Jefferson, agreed. But France was attacking American ships and demanding money in exchange for peace talks. This caused many Americans to call for war against France.

John felt France was treating the United States "neither as allies nor as friends, nor as a sovereign state." He decided to prepare for war while continuing to press for peace.

John also approved laws that allowed the government to expel foreigners it felt were "dangerous to the peace and safety of the United States." The government could also punish people who wrote or spoke out against it. Jefferson was strongly opposed to these laws.

John's peace efforts succeeded, but he lost the election of 1800. Jefferson became the new president.

This portrait of John was painted in 1798 during his term as president.

Retiring to Write

John and Abigail settled down on their farm for good. John loved being back on the land. He devoted himself to reading, writing, and farming.

In 1812, he started corresponding again with his old friend and political foe, Jefferson. "You and I ought not to die, before we have explained ourselves to each other," he wrote. During the next fourteen years, the two exchanged 158 letters and eventually reconciled their differences.

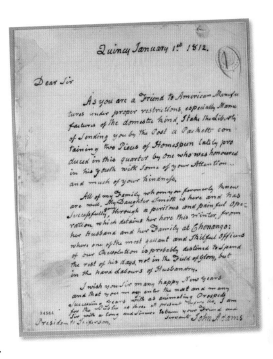

On October 28, 1818, Abigail died. John grieved the loss of the woman he called "my dearest friend." He lived to see his son John Quincy become president in 1825. The following year, on July 4, 1826, John died— just a few hours after Thomas Jefferson's death.

This portrait of John Adams was painted in London in 1783. Abigail Adams called it "a very good likeness" of her husband. The scroll in his hand may be the Treaty of Paris. On the table is a map of America.

Analyze the Subject

- John Adams was a firm believer in the right of the American colonies to be independent from Great Britain. Identify two examples that show his conviction.
- What were some of Adams's contributions to American independence?
- Who were some of the most important people in Adams's life?

Focus on Comprehension:
Text Structure and Organization

- The author uses sequence-of-events text structure to organize this biography. She uses both dates and words. Identify two examples of dates and two examples of words that show this structure.
- Reread "Farm Boy." What text structure does the author use for this section?
- Reread "Rebellion Grows." The author uses multiple cause-and-effect text structures for this section. Explain how.

Analyze the Tools Writers Use: Direct Quotes

- The author uses a direct quote from John Adams to describe how he felt about being vice president. Adams called it "the most insignificant office that ever the invention of man contrived." Did the author pick a quote that makes it easy for readers to know how Adams felt about being vice president? Why or why not?
- What else does the quote tell you about Adams? Was he a good speaker?

Tips for Interpreting Text Structure

Cause and Effect/Problem and Solution words include **because, so, as a result, therefore**, and **consequently**.

Compare and Contrast words include **however, but, too, on the other hand**, and **instead**.

Sequence/Steps in a Process words include specific dates, **first, after, then, finally, now, later**, and **not long after**.

Description words include **also, in fact, for instance**, details, and sense words.

Focus on Words: Emotion Words

Make a chart like the one below. Locate each word in the biography. Read sentences around the word and determine a possible definition using context clues. Check the definition in a dictionary. Finally, ask yourself, *Whom or what is the emotion word describing?*

Page	Word	Dictionary Definition	Whom the Word Is Describing
7	irritable		
8	enraged		
9	dismayed		
11	somber		
13	frustrated		

The Boston Tea Party

Abigail Adams

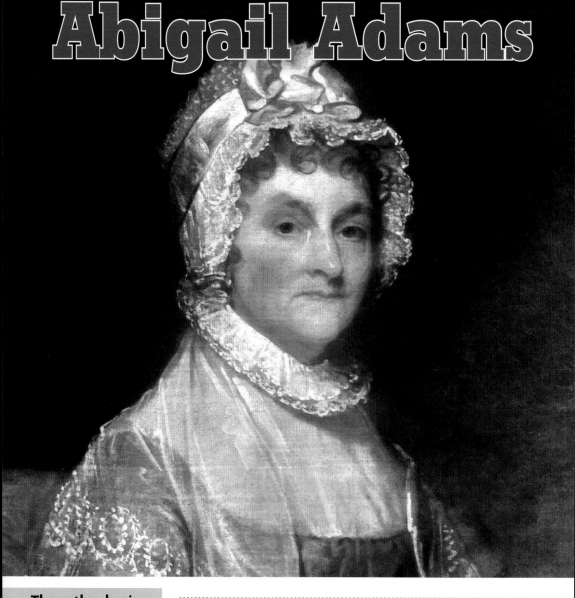

The author begins with a strong hook: a direct quote from the subject about her feelings for her country. Abigail Adams comes off as a strong-minded patriot whom readers will want to get to know.

I would not exchange my country . . . or be any other than an American, though I might be queen or empress of any nation," wrote Abigail Adams in a letter to her husband, John, in May 1778.

Abigail was very proud of both her husband and her country. She **suffered** many long separations from him as he helped to build the nation. John also hated to be apart from the woman he called his "best, dearest, worthiest, wisest friend in this world." But Abigail was sure that their sacrifices were part of their patriotic duty. Their love for each other and their nation supported them for more than fifty years.

A Smart and Stubborn Girl

Abigail Smith was born on November 11, 1744, in Weymouth, Massachusetts. She grew up in a lively household that included three other children. Her father was a church minister. Her mother kept house and cared for sick people in the community.

The author provides the date and place of Abigail's birth and her maiden name, Smith.

Like all colonial girls, Abigail had many chores to do. Her mother taught her how to cook, sew, and clean. She learned how to make soap, keep chickens, tend a garden, and milk a cow. She also learned to read, write, and do arithmetic. Abigail **longed** to go to school but, like many colonial girls, was educated at home by her mother. Her father also encouraged her to read the many books in his library. He taught her to ask questions about what she read and to discuss ideas.

The author gives details about the subject's childhood.

Abigail freely shared her strong opinions and **stubbornly** defended them. This worried her mother, who thought she was unladylike. But Abigail's grandmother just chuckled and said, "Wild colts make the best horses."

The author tells about important people in the subject's life. Readers learn that from an early age, Abigail was encouraged to have and to voice her own ideas and opinions on issues. Understanding her upbringing will help inform readers of her life, and accomplishments, as an adult.

Abigail was born in this house, which still stands in the town of Weymouth, Massachusetts.

Abigail and John Together

Abigail met John Adams when she was about fifteen. They married a few years later on October 25, 1764, and lived in the house next door to John's childhood home.

John's work as a lawyer kept him busy. Abigail was just as busy running the farm and home. Soon she was also busy raising a child: Their first child, Nabby, was born in 1765. Two years later, Abigail gave birth to son John Quincy.

The little family's happiness contrasted with the unrest in the colonies caused by disagreements with the far-off British government. By 1768, John was caught up in protests against Great Britain. To make it easier for him to work and to go to political meetings, the Adams family moved to Boston.

At first, Abigail liked living in the city. But she did not like hearing British troops marching near their home. The troops had been placed in Boston as a way of warning colonists not to stir up any trouble.

The troops made Abigail nervous. But like many other colonial women, she continued to protest British policies by boycotting British goods. She worked hard to keep her family clothed and fed.

In December 1768, Abigail gave birth to another daughter, Susanna. She devotedly cared for the weak, sickly baby, but Susanna died about a year later. Abigail and John were **brokenhearted**.

Trouble in Boston

In March 1770, the Boston Massacre added to their sadness. When John defended the British soldiers accused of shooting colonists, Abigail supported him. But she also feared for his life at the hands of an angry mob. Abigail had even more to fear when John was elected to the Massachusetts legislature. Taking this job marked him as a rebel in the eyes of the British government.

Abigail herself rebelled by continuing to boycott British tea. She knew that in some cities, colonists had refused even to unload tea from ships. So she figured there would be trouble when three cargo ships arrived in Boston Harbor in December 1773.

The author shows different sides of Abigail's personality: She was supportive of her husband, and a daring rebel herself.

21

Abigail and John corresponded often. This letter from Abigail describes the Battle of Bunker Hill.

This direct quote from Abigail shows her skill as a writer, and also helps readers get a feeling for her as a person.

"The tea, that baneful weed, is arrived. Great, and I hope effectual, opposition has been made to the landing of it," she wrote to a friend. She was pleased when she heard that patriots had tossed the tea into the harbor. But rebellious Boston no longer felt like a safe place to raise her family, which now included two more boys, Charles and Thomas. By summer, the Adamses had moved back to their farm.

Abigail Runs the Farm

On August 10, 1774, Abigail waved good-bye to John as he set off on a 400-mile journey to Philadelphia, Pennsylvania, to attend the First Continental Congress.

Abigail was proud of John, but sorry to see him go. Within days, she sent him a letter that began, "It seems already a month since you left me. The great anxiety I feel for my country, for you, and for our family renders the day tedious and the night unpleasant."

This letter was among the first of hundreds that Abigail and John would exchange during the next three years. Abigail's letters provided John with important news about events in Boston. John shared her information with other representatives. "I think you shine as a stateswoman of late, as well as a farmeress," he wrote to her.

Abigail was indeed a good "farmeress." On her own, she ran the farm and raised the children. She rented out land and took care of the family's money matters. She fed and sheltered people who fled Boston after British soldiers took it over.

Abigail also witnessed battles between colonists and British troops. She watched one battle from a hilltop on June 17, 1775. "The day—perhaps the decisive day—is come, on which the fate of America depends," she wrote.

By spring of 1776, many colonists were convinced that America must declare independence from Great Britain.

> The author again quotes Abigail. Her use of various emotion words shows mixed feelings about her husband attending the First Continental Congress: She is proud of John, sad he is gone, anxious about the situation, and finds the time without him boring and unpleasant.

> The author shows that Abigail was a strong and capable individual, not just the wife of a political figure.

23

The author shows that Abigail was surprisingly modern in her thinking, a quality that readers of the biography will respect. It also gives them a better understanding of how she impacted the world then, and why we still read about her today.

Abigail wanted John not only to work for independence, but also to consider equal rights for women. She wrote, ". . . in the new code of laws . . . I desire you would remember the ladies and be more generous and favorable to them than your ancestors."

Abigail cooked in this kitchen to feed family and friends while John was away.

The Adams Family in Europe

Abigail's dearest wish was for her family to be together. Yet she was happy for John when he was sent to France as a representative, though it meant another long separation. She supported his decision to take John Quincy with him.

Father and son left on February 15, 1778. Abigail would not see them again until they returned in June 1779, and then it was only briefly. Five months later, John set sail for Europe once more, this time with both John Quincy and Charles.

Four years passed. Abigail did a fine job running the farm, but she missed John terribly. She wrote to him often. Finally, in July 1784, Abigail and Nabby traveled to Europe themselves.

At first, John, Abigail, and their children lived in a big house near Paris, France. Abigail thought Paris was a "horrid dirty city," but she liked seeing plays in its theaters. Less than a year later, the Adamses moved to London, England. Abigail thought the English countryside was pretty, but she longed to return to America. She wrote that "retiring to our own little farm, feeding my poultry and improving my garden has more charms" than living in Europe.

The author describes a key period in Abigail's life: living in Europe. For her time, Abigail was a celebrity.

The Second First Lady

In 1788, Abigail got her wish. She, John, and Nabby returned to Massachusetts. But soon after they settled into their home, John was elected the nation's first vice president! By summer 1789, Abigail and John were living near New York City, the nation's first capital.

As the vice president's wife, Abigail had to host many formal dinners. All this had to be done with little money, but Abigail was used to budgeting. A year later, she **endured** moving yet again, this time to Philadelphia. She organized the packing despite becoming sick in the process.

When John won a second term as vice president in 1792, Abigail decided to live on their farm instead of in Philadelphia. She was worn out and often in poor health. Once again she managed the farm and cared for the family.

But when John won the presidency in the 1796 election, Abigail knew she had to be by his side. "I never wanted your advice and assistance more in my life," John wrote to her. She finally arrived in Philadelphia in May 1797.

As the nation's "first lady," Abigail once again hosted large dinner parties. She gave John advice and supported him when newspapers criticized him. But she felt sad that the nation did not seem to appreciate John's hard work.

The author tells about another important event in Abigail's life: She and John were the first couple to ever live in the White House in Washington, D.C. It was still under construction!

Her final job as first lady was to turn the White House in Washington, D.C., into a home. The city was still being built in 1800, and the big house was not yet finished. There was scarcely any furniture, and the plaster walls were still wet. Abigail hung laundry to dry in the largest space, which would one day be the elegant East Room.

The sight of enslaved African people laboring to build the city saddened Abigail. She and John had long opposed slavery. She felt that African workers had "as good a right to freedom" as colonists did.

"We Retire from Public Life"

When John lost the election in November 1800, Abigail looked forward to living on her farm again. Her only hope was that the nation would enjoy the "peace, happiness, and prosperity" it had under Washington and Adams.

John Quincy Adams

Abigail died at the farm on October 28, 1818. John Quincy summed up his mother's life with these words: "She had been fifty-four years the delight of my father's heart, the sweetener of all his toils, the comforter of all his sorrows, the sharer and heightener of all his joys."

The author concludes with a quote (from her son) about the subject of the biography. Hearing others' words about Abigail Adams helps readers gain an appreciation of her life and work.

In 2003, Abigail was honored with a life-size statue that stands on the Commonwealth Avenue Mall in Boston, Massachusetts.

Analyze the Subject

- Abigail Adams was an intelligent and capable woman and a true partner to her husband, John Adams. Identify two examples of how Abigail helped John and her family.
- What were some of Abigail's biggest accomplishments?
- What were some of Abigail's greatest challenges?

Focus on Comprehension: Text Structure and Organization

- The author uses sequence-of-events text structure to organize this biography. She uses both dates and words. Identify two examples of dates and two examples of words that show this structure.
- Reread "Abigail and John Together." What sequence-of-events word does the author use in this section?
- Reread "Abigail Runs the Farm." What text structure does the author use to tell us about Abigail being a good "farmeress"?

Focus on Motif

Authors often use recurring themes, or ideas, in stories. Recurring themes are called **motifs**. What is the motif for this story?

Analyze the Tools Writers Use: Direct Quotes

- The author uses this direct quote from a letter Abigail Adams wrote to her husband as the colonies were preparing to declare their independence from Great Britain: ". . . in the new code of laws . . . I desire you would remember the ladies and be more generous and favorable to them than your ancestors." What does this quote tell you about how Abigail Adams felt about women's rights?
- Considering the time in the history of the country that she wrote it, what else does this quote tell you about Abigail Adams?

Focus on Words: Emotion Words

Make a chart like the one below. Locate each word in the biography.
Read sentences around the word and determine a possible definition
using context clues and the dictionary. Finally, ask yourself, *Whom or what
is the emotion word describing?*

Page	Word	Dictionary Definition	Whom the Word Is Describing
18	suffered		
19	longed		
19	stubbornly		
21	brokenhearted		
26	endured		

How does an author write a

BIOGRAPHY?

Reread "Abigail Adams" and think about what the author did to write this biography. How did she describe Abigail Adams's life? How did she show what Abigail Adams accomplished?

1. Decide on Someone to Write About

Remember: A biography is a factual retelling of someone's life. Therefore, you must research his or her life and, if possible, interview the person. In "Abigail Adams," the author wants to show readers that Abigail Adams was not only John Adams's wife but also a very intelligent and capable woman, whom he regarded as his greatest supporter and friend.

2. Decide Who Else Needs to Be in the Biography

Other people will likely be an important part of your subject's life. Ask yourself:

• Who was in the person's family?
• Who were the person's friends and neighbors?
• Whom did the person go to school with or work with?
• Who helped or hurt the person?
• Which people should I include?
• How will I describe these people?

Person or Group	How They Impacted Abigail Adams's Life
father	taught Abigail to read, write, and do arithmetic; encouraged her to have opinions about what she read and to discuss ideas
mother	taught Abigail how to care for a house and a farm
John Adams	appreciated his wife, Abigail, for her intelligence and capabilities; was her best friend and the nation's first vice president and second president

3. Recall Events and Setting

Jot down notes about what happened in the subject's life and where these things happened. Ask yourself:

- Where did the person's experiences take place? How will I describe these places?
- What were the most important events in his or her life?
- What situations or problems did the person experience?
- What did the person accomplish?
- What questions might my readers have about the subject that I could answer in my biography?

Subject	Setting(s)	Important Events
Abigail Adams	the American colonies, later the United States; France; England	1. She learns to read, write, and do arithmetic and to take care of a home and a farm while still a child. 2. She marries John Adams in 1764. 3. She boycotts British tea to protest high taxes. 4. She manages the family farm while John is at the Continental Congress. 5. She travels to France and England to be with John, who is there on government business. 6. She moves into the White House with John when he is president; they are the first couple to live there.

Glossary

brokenhearted (BROH-ken-HAR-ted) extremely sad (page 21)

dismayed (dis-MADE) disappointed and confused (page 9)

endured (in-DOORD) experienced the hardship of something (page 26)

enraged (in-RAJED) filled with anger (page 8)

frustrated (FRUS-tray-ted) discouraged and upset (page 13)

irritable (EER-ih-tuh-bul) short-tempered (page 7)

longed (LAUNGD) wanted strongly (page 19)

somber (SAHM-ber) serious (page 11)

stubbornly (STUH-bern-lee) obstinately unyielding (page 19)

suffered (SUH-ferd) had to put up with difficult circumstances (page 18)